A Woman in Progress

poems

Barbara Marie Minney

Sheila-Na-Gig Editions

A Woman In Progress ©2024 Barbara Marie Minney

Cover image: iStock/Liudmyla Supynska

Author photo: Melanie Rae Buonavolonta

ISBN: 978-1-962405-00-3

Sheila-Na-Gig Editions
Russell, KY
Hayley Mitchell Haugen, Editor
www.sheilanagigblog.com

ADVANCE PRAISE

Barbara Marie Minney's fourth book of poetry, *A Woman in Progress*, is a gem. It not only outlines but conveys the soul of their story of transformation—warts and all. Their poetry grabs you by the scruff of your neck, draws you into their experience, and helps you understand the depth of their emotions, and the courage it took to begin their journey. And a journey it is, one such as the majority of us never have or will experience, other than through Barbara's intimate sharing of their words. A MUST READ for those who wish to have a greater understanding.

—Doc Janning, Inaugural Poet Laureate of South Euclid, Ohio

Barbara Marie Minney presents us with a slim volume of expansive work. *A Woman in Progress* certainly speaks in ways that might surprise each reader: lines that resonate deeply, or the turn of a phrase that catches us unaware. Or the revelations and resolutions that speak to a life being lived authentically. In "Rainbow on the Bathroom Rug: Akron Pride," Minney tells us of her "chance to rejoice in my own uniqueness." Indeed, the entirety of the collection speaks to a life running headlong into recognizing, accepting, and embracing her uniqueness. The opening poem "No Experience Needed," perfectly sets the scene for the reader, as she shows us that Barbara Marie Minney is boldly claiming her path through life through her words. I've been moved, changed even, by her work.

— M. Lynne Squires, Pushcart Prize-nominated author of *Letters to My Son: Reflections of Appalachia at Mid-Century.*

ACKNOWLEDGMENTS

Grateful acknowledgment is given to the following publications in which these poems first appeared, sometimes in slightly different versions:

"A Woman in Progress" is an erasure poem. The primary source material is Erin Joy Henry's essay "Embracing Womanhood: Why I'm Still A Work in Progress" (*Huffington Post*, 10/13/2011). The first and last parts of the poem are my own words.

I Thought I Heard A Cardinal Sing: "Rainbow on the Bathroom Rug: Akron Pride"

Love Poems Anthology and Silver Birch Press: "Tomato Sandwich"

"Masochistic Murmurs" is a found poem. The primary sources are *Whipping Girl: A Transexual Woman on Sexism and the Scapegoating of Femininity* by Julia Serano (Seal Press, 2007 and 2016); *Screw the Roses, Give Me the Thorns: The Romance and Sexual Sorcery of Sadomasochism* by Philip Miller and Molly Devon (Mystic Rose Books, 1995 and 2003); and *The Holy Bible.*

National Benevolent Association Called to Care eNewsletter: "Silent Suffering"

new words issue one: "Talk to Me"

Of Rust and Glass Pride: "Dancing Naked Pantoum," "No Experience Needed"

Poetic Memoir Chapbook Challenge: a portion of "Psychiatrists Are (Not) For Sissies"

To Marilyn, wife, lover, best friend, soulmate, muse, forever my first and last reader, editor, manager, adviser, critic, and co-conspirator. You taught me how to be a woman.

CONTENTS

No Experience Needed

Lurking naked in the shadows, she said,
"You don't have enough life experiences to be a serious poet,"
the blue green of her daybreak eyes polished
by the dawn,
moonlight hair dark as raven feathers.

Never a lonesome cowboy riding the range.
Never a revolutionary working for change.
Never a matador killing bulls in Spain.
Never a battered junkie shooting cocaine.
Never a weary janitor cleaning floors.
Never a sneaky john cruising for whores.
Never a pregnant hitchhiker on the road.
Never a debonair spy speaking in code.
Never an ambulance driver wounded in war.
Never a ragged castaway washed ashore.
Never a homeless train hopping hobo.
Never a vagrant wino on skid row.
Never a seasick merchant seaman.
Never a soldier in the French Foreign Legion.
Never a hot rod racer on the track.
Never a lonely hermit living in a shack.
Never a washed up boxer in the ring.
Never a brutal mercenary in Beijing.
Never a secret member of a sleeper cell.
Never a derelict thrown in a redneck jail.

"I did change genders," I said quietly.
"Does that count for anything?"

A Woman in Progress
—with excerpts from Erin Joy Henry

In the dungeon,
   I am cuffed to the St. Andrew's cross,
he is standing behind,
   flogger wielding master,
accusatory eyes burning through the hood
   cock straining against leather pants
storm raging with each stroke
   on my bare ass.

   in awe of women

     expressing   feelings and emotions

           I could pull over my face completely

   to make me want to vomit.

     dormant   for   years

there was   no crying in life.

       this feminine creature inside

   demanded to express herself.

not allowed to enter   temples and sacred places I was there to
explore.

    walked around in shame

           I hid

until

surrounded

by a loving essence so strong I   actually see it.

somehow able to   apply love to all the

places inside   that hurt.

honor my feminine as sacred.

the key

to survival.

let go of self judgment

value   vulnerability. Showing up as your authentic self

In the dungeon,
he is tied to the St. Andrew's cross,
bare ass exposed
cock not so hard now.
I am standing behind,
flogger in my hand.
I am the dominatrix.
I am in charge
I am the storm.

October 7, 2018
—for Marilyn

I cling to the tear-filled Kleenex in my hand,
holding it like a lifeline,
just like I've clung to you
through all these years,
like an addict clings to his blood-stained needle
feeling the surge of relief through his veins

just like Peter Cetera sang
"You're a Hard Habit to Break"
…not that I ever wanted to,
it would have been worse than
Lennon's "Cold Turkey"
…and that was a pretty bad song

how am I ever going to
get through these seven pages
of vows I have written,
yes, sometimes I get wordy
…after all I was trained to be a lawyer

we are like opposite ends of a battery
…you positive
…me negative,
you always could peel me back
like the layers of an onion
until the blue-violet tears flow like dirty wine

these are not tears of sadness
…but tears of joy
that you are still here after thirty-seven years,
sometimes I felt like you didn't really love me
…you just tolerated me
until something better came along

that was my internal struggle
not yours
...my self-pity
...my distrust
...my fortifications
against my own demons

you always stayed above the fray,
stable and strong as bedrock,
while I took for granted things
never said or understood

I lost count of the number of times
you saved me,
like a saint in shining armor
fighting the dragons of despair
...and I fought dragons for you, too,
they were just smaller.

Tomato Sandwich

It's simple really,
a red ripe Marietta tomato
cut into slices,
placed between two pieces of bread,
add a little mayo,
and you have a tomato sandwich.

But, there is much more
to it than that,
memories garnish those wedges of bread
formed and to be formed,
consumed and to be consumed
just like the sandwiches,
the nectar tickling my chin.

Brushing against the earthy herbal scent
of grandma's tomato plants,
carefully staked in neat rows,
in the small field
next to the old wooden outhouse,
a two-seater with last year's
Sears and Roebuck Christmas catalog toilet paper,
always wondering if the location
made the tomatoes grow better,
the lusty smell of the outhouse mingling with
the warm savory scent of the plants
creating the aroma of summer
and tomatoes yet to come.

I don't have kids to share these stories with,
but I have a wife,
citified, but the love of my life,
maybe the only person

I've ever really loved,
or who has ever really loved me back.

Love dies easily for me
and it is always a hard birth,
sometimes even a stillbirth,
but there is always the one
that was brought to me as if by wonder,
picnicking by a quivering brook,
the only one that I share my tomato sandwich with.

41

—to commemorate our 41st anniversary

and I don't mean George H.W. Bush. I mean us. Two
fragmented Sgt. Pepper's Lonely Hearts. Stimulated and
inspired by diverse elements. Cross-pollinated into one queer
variety.

I want to bleed poetry for you
shout alleluia until my lungs explode
sweat psalms of thanksgiving and praise.

Youth like an out of focus photograph. Glazed over by time.
Raising our heads toward heaven in veneration. Sentient
shadows seeking the mind asylum. Souls colliding on
moonbeams.

Beauty out of chaos
creating our own divine presence
pieces of our selves forever in the other's heart.

Motionless in the Amish bed and breakfast. Kissing deeply and
honestly. Eleven on the McDonald's pickle scale. Claiming our
transformative love. A revolutionary act.

You said you loved me very much. Space stilled. Time stopped.
Lightning in a snowstorm. Radiant light miracle.

For the first time
after all these years
I finally believed it.

Yearning for Salt

I want to taste salted moths
    recklessness wet on my tongue

bathe in pickle brine
    strong enough to bear up an egg

fresh green cucumbers float like toy boats.
    Bright lamp chimneys

shimmer in my parched throat
    keeping the fire going

to taste the smell of her.

Depression Poems

#1

A basket overflowing with unanswered shoulds
sinks down forlornly in the corner,

Western Union boys delivering painful rejections
lie in wait at the door,

flowers unblooming in the spilled spaghetti sauce,
icy promises squirm on broken plates.

#2

A marooned whale struggles
on jagged rocks

aimless and adrift,
out of its world,

estranged from
its evolutionary trajectory.

#3

I swallowed lightning glass
a discharge of electricity
cutting holes

in my belly. A shock wave
of expanding explosions in
my negatively charged

storm cloud brain. Out among
the doomed and the damned
losing control of the wrongness.

#4

crushed under the wheels of a truck
    madness one steering wheel turn away

a cacophony sinkhole of confusion
    salsa taste of vengeance bitter in the mouth

out among the dragons
    painful guttural groan forming in the throat

stepping over the bullshit
    finding queer comfort in self-isolation

#5

I just read *Auguries of Innocence* by Patti Smith.
I did not understand any of it.
Why is poetry considered to be great
    so hard to decipher?

What's the point?

My poetry will never
    reach those heights.
In that game, I am a scrub
    forever sitting at
the end of the bench.

The wind blows away from me,
aroma of rejection sour on the tongue
hanging on by a loose thread
from the noose around my neck.

#6

The feverish frenzy of the storm
drains the lifeblood from the sea
like a radioactive mosquito.

White horses stampede across
beach toes, more turbulent
with each feral breath.

A church mouse high on cannabis
chases a cat around the sanctuary
while broken-hearted

Victorian maidens silently pray,
snarls smelling like broken dreams
escaping from lipstick-stained teeth.

#7
(Broken Stalks)

It must be a psychoactive dream. Field crowned by an oceanic
abyss of gilded wheat. Eager to be harvested. Dark haired Mail
Pouch Tobacco barns diffusing dots between wind waves.
Spittoons of moonless nights.

Combines only reap the easy. Stalks standing straight up. Rolling
over the bent, broken, and beaten. Twisted and crushed flat into
the ground. Ignored, marginalized, and soulless. Brain-dead

zombies sweating blood. Shuffling through a personal universe. Trampled, trashed, and tokenized.

Hysterically screaming in a wasteland purgatory. Staring unblinkingly into the sun. Looking for a message that isn't there. Intimidated by emotion. Wishing my soul could sing.

Am I too broken to be saved?

Psychiatrists Are (Not) for Sissies

—Lyrical Essay

I sat in the chair in your cramped office on the 4th floor of St. Thomas Hospital. You did not even have a couch to lie on. You fit me into your schedule at the request of my doctor. I was referred to you for ECT, which you said I did not need. That may have been the only benefit from the time we spent together. You didn't believe in medication either. Just talk, talk, and talk about Dad.

Talking to you was like talking to my grandfather. Who wants to talk to their grandfather about sex and gender? Topics that you admitted you knew nothing about after two years. All you wanted to hear about were my dreams. When I went to bed, it was like you were a voyeur hovering over me as I slept and dreamt. It was kind of creepy, but I believed that you could help.

I wouldn't let you corkscrew too far into my head. Maybe that's why you didn't help me. Just dreams about Dad, which you admitted you could not even interpret.

The cat was always sitting
on the bookshelf,
looking at me with
her smug cat smirk
as if I were a mouse
to be toyed with,
gleaming with the power
of the pussy,
a radioactive feline.

Can you have the power
if you don't have a pussy?

Hemingway is my literary hero. Not his toxic machismo. I admire the way he died. I once told you I wanted to take a selfie with Hemingway. You asked if that was a dream. I said no.

Living with authenticity,
boldly and truly,
as a charging lion
with a little too much testosterone.

Instead of blowing my brains out
I only killed part of myself,
switching genders
with Papa frowning,
the one true sentence of my life.

I have lived most of my life being what others wanted me to be. Now that I am closer to death than birth, I want to feel like I'm living for myself. I have experienced anxiety and depression and even contemplated suicide. I looked at suicide as a romantic way to die. I once asked a psychic if she thought I would die by suicide. She said no one had ever asked her that question before. Then, she answered no, but hedged her bet by adding unless I was ill, and the pain became overwhelming. She added that I did not fear suicide.

The psychic also said that my book of life is heavy, but the pages turn easily and that I was put on this earth to do exactly what I am doing. That is comforting, if it is true. She had no interest in my dreams. Instead, she recounted her dreams of me.

I once had a dream in which Dad looked exactly like Bob Dylan on the cover of the *New Morning* album, but he really couldn't sing except in the shower. Well, on second thought, maybe he did sing as good as Dylan. Dad shows up frequently in my dreams. I'm certain he died with a lot of regrets. I do not want to be like Dad.

I was born older than my years
no other choice but to be
an adult on arrival,

childhood packed away in earthenware jars
hidden in remote caves of imagination
like the Dead Sea Scrolls,
fragments waiting to be unearthed.

An impostor bluffing through
a role intended for someone else,
performing like a washed-up actor,
reciting lines written in blood,
toy props scattered across the stage,
still six years old and
at the mercy of my long dead father.

For a highly educated man, Dad was a racist. He received a Ph.D. The first and probably only person in his family to do so. My brother and I would tease him by asking him to say something philosophical.

His idea of equality was to spare no race or ethnicity from ridicule. I'm ashamed to admit, I repeated some of his jokes. In 1978, on my first day as an assistant prosecutor in a rural Ohio county, the chief investigator gave me a cartoon of a target superimposed over an African American man. You can probably guess where the bulls-eye was. I left it in my desk for my successor when I left. I guess that I did become like Dad.

Dad went into a nursing home and immediately went on a hunger strike. Six weeks later, he was dead. I was in the car on my way to visit him two hours away when I got the call. I did not give them permission to move him until I got there. He looked so small and frail, his skin almost luminescent, as he laid on a soiled bedsheet. I kissed him on the head.

Talk to Me

The Queen in the bathtub. Shattering the glass cage. Clowns wearing pork pie hats. Speaking in Oxford accents. Girls promenading in the street with yellow tulips. Beatniks listening to Bird. Talking hipster lingo. Nodding off in a kaleidoscopic haze. Sharp smells of old wine and urine. Sinner and saint sharing the same empty grave in Garrettsville. Horizon so very far away. No more fucks left to give.

Not drunk like Hart Crane
feeling an urge to jump ship
converse with the sea.

The Silence Finds its Way to Me

The silence finds its way to me
    as the wrinkled man
        beaten and withdrawn
sits on the worn park bench
    fountains smiling in his head.
Pulling a scarf of quietude around me
    I dream beyond the
        boundaries of my imagination
and like Chinese demons
    travel on a straight line
toward smiles of delicious pleasure
    as silky desire
        heats my soul.

Silent Suffering

Frozen silence entombs
the spirit

in a frigid mausoleum

Refracted sunlight
reflects a canvas of hopelessness

in a surge of finality

Success insignificant
buried as if it never existed

in a hole that will never be filled

A lemming
throwing itself

in a canyon of warped thinking

Dragging itself along a path
that goes

in the direction of nowhere

Avoiding harmful things
only increases anxiety

in what may be missed

Hopefulness fragile
like a porcelain doll shattered

in a thousand pieces

Desperately clinging to the normality bridge
daring to plunge

in an expanse of monomaniacal intensity

Confused by not wanting to die
but not wanting to be here anymore either

in that void of nothingness

Beseeching a nonexistent god
to be stronger than the melancholy

and

in believing it

let's talk about suicide...

Naomi Judd and Kate Spade
made the headlines

what about all the clinched fist brains
of invisible people grasping

that spear point of hopelessness
in the solitude and loneliness

strangling their minds

i've been there

yet I did not pull the trigger
take the pills or walk
in the water with stones in my pocket

why me

Rainbow on the Bathroom Rug: Akron Pride

I've lived a whole lifetime as someone I wasn't.

Wandering through gender-sensitive backcountry, from
the hills and hollers of West Virginia,
the grasslands and cornfields of Ohio,
through Stonewall and Pulse,
making it to Akron

like my Appalachian kinsfolk
during the great exodus north,
on the hillbilly highway,
looking for a better life
in the rubber factories
of Goodyear, Goodrich, Firestone.

I was searching for something too,
not knowing what it was.

      The rainbow appeared suddenly,
      the afternoon sun's reflection on
      the bathroom rug,
      a sign that

      I had chased the rainbow logic,
      revealing myself
      on the other side,
      more treasured than any
      pot of Leprechaun gold.

Coming together
for one day
celebrating our diversity,
letting the world know

we have survived another year,
we are still here,
we are not going away,

a chance to rejoice in my own uniqueness,
a chance to cry

a sacred experience
like a dream sequence
fading into misty haze
the crowd cheering for
the choices I have made.
I may have wandered through
a lifetime
as someone I wasn't,
now in whatever time I have left on this earth,
I'm home.

Masochistic Murmurs
—with excerpts from Julia Serano, Philip Miller and Molly Devon,
and *The Holy Bible*

My culture had its way with me
    in ways that I will never understand,
my self-esteem ripped right out of me

    now all that's left is a submissive streak.

I turned to the rest of the world to
    figure out who I was

what I was worth

a masochist who derives pleasure
    by receiving pain
in a beautiful but twisted way
    like the unnamed narrator in *Venus in Furs.*

Surrendering control of herself into
    the hands of the dominant world
like a good little boy
    obeying earthly masters with fear and trembling,

presenting my body as a living sacrifice.
    Picking up on all of the not so-subliminal messages

like TV shows where father knows best
    fairy tales where helpless girls
await a handsome prince
    and cartoons where superman always saves Lois Lane.

Hospitals wrap baby girls in pink flannel blankets
    and boys get blue ones

schoolyard taunts like "sissy" and "fairy" and "pussy"
all teach that feminine is synonymous with weakness.
Nobody needed to tell me that I
should be bound and flagellated for
wanting to be the lesser sex.
To satisfy her need

a natural female submissive recognizes
her earthborn inclinations.

Sexuality became a strange
combination of jealousy, self-loathing, and guilt
my brain concocting fantasies
right out of BDSM handbooks.

Mental library full of erotic cerebral cinema,
provocative images and language
gathered from imagined experiences
woven into the labyrinth of my sexuality.

Private parts responding to conditioning
coming face-to-face with my own misogyny
unlearning lessons that were etched into my psyche
before I ever set foot in school.

The attraction for the submissive is
freedom to let go,
removing the stumbling blocks
to experience pleasure,

no longer alone in a hostile universe.

Looking into my own eyes
finding endless strength
and inconsolable sadness

overcoming humiliation and abuse,
feeling shame for my desires
but having the courage
to pursue them anyway
appreciating how fucking empowering

it can be to be female,

a sign that I am finally beginning
to learn to love myself.

Dancing Naked Pantoum

I once bought porn on a Sunday school trip,
being naughty was the most delicious thing.
Building an island around conformity
was the greatest of all gifts I could bring.

Being naughty was the most delicious thing,
in the duskiness of the club, dance floor murky,
I was the greatest of all gifts I could bring
oscillating with the breath of sweat and yearning.

In the club's duskiness, dance floor murky,
edges smear like a mirage, gyrating DJ
oscillating with the breath of sweat and yearning
apparition, in the time expanse, the crowd at bay.

Smearing edges like a mirage, gyrating DJ
guitar shredding, drums bruising *Transgender Dysphoria Blues*
in the time expanse, an apparition, the crowd at bay
buzz sawing rhythmic eruptions through my shoes.

Transgender Dysphoria Blues shredded by guitars, bruised by drums,
costume dragged over my head just as Laura Jane Grace sings
rhythmic eruptions buzz sawing through my shoes
voice carried to my ears on serpent's wings.

Costume dragged over my head just as Laura Jane Grace sings
"You want them to notice the ragged ends of your summer dress,"
serpent's wings carry her voice to my ears,
breasts caressing air, aroused nipples provoking the beat.

"You want them to notice the ragged ends of your summer dress"
tracing light rays from winking strobe lights,
breasts caressing air, aroused nipples provoking the beat
others receding into senseless rapture nights.

I once bought porn on a Sunday school trip,
provoking thoughts of liberation that have been,
tracing light rays from winking strobe lights
penis hardening into an encouraging grin.

Barbara Marie Minney is a transgender woman, award winning poet, writer, speaker, teaching artist, and quiet activist. Her poetry and essays have appeared in numerous publications, including *Politico, The Buckeye Flame, The Gasconade Review, Gargoyle Magazine, The Pine Cone Review, Women Speak: Women of Appalachia Project, Woman Scream: The International Poetry Anthology of Female Voices, The New Wasteland, new words (issue one): a trans and gender-expansive journal,* and *I Thought I Heard A Cardinal Sing, Ohio's Appalachian Voices.* Barbara's poetry has also been translated into Spanish. She is the author of *If There's No Heaven,* the winner of the 2020 Poetry Is Life Book Award and an *Akron Beacon Journal* Best Northeast Ohio Book in 2020; the *Poetic Memoir Chapbook Challenge;* and *Dance Naked With God.* Barbara is a retired attorney and a seventh-generation Appalachian and lives in Tallmadge, Ohio, with her wife of over 42 years and a menagerie of stuffed animals. You can follow Barbara at https://www.barbaramarieminneypoetry.com.

Sheila-Na-Gig Editions